Missed Chances

For Megan
with best wishes
Sam Adams

Missed Chances

SAM ADAMS

ACKNOWLEDGEMENTS

With a few exceptions, the poems that appear in the following pages have been published previously. Grateful acknowledgement is made to the editors of the journals in which they appeared: *Poetry Wales*, *PN Review*, *Planet*, *The New Welsh Review*, and *The Western Mail*.

ISBN: 0 86243 864 0
ISBN-13: 9780862438647

Printed and published in Wales
by Y Lolfa Cyf., Talybont, Ceredigion SY24 5AP
e-mail ylolfa@ylolfa.com
website www.ylolfa.com
tel. (01970) 832 304

For Muriel

Contents

Kite Flying

On days of noisy wind that combs
The rippling grasses this way and that
As it passes, and tugs at clothes

With sly unbuttoning fingers
And takes the breath away, I think
How we would lie in some drowned hollow

While the slow kite wriggled in its stream.
How sad that some boys never learn
To fly a kite. I thought that I

Should never get it right – perhaps
I had made my cross too rigid,
Perhaps my paste and paper were too frail.

We knew those moments when the breeze
Would fail our fledgling project
And the taut held line would sag,

But we launched out sweetly on the air
Again and cast off twine enough
To let our hobby climb and climb.

Bird Strike

In the spring I watched the earthbound
Creatures nesting, tending no young,
Coming and going;
I heard sounds of their living,
The mingling of unmusical voices.

They worked the garden too,
But could not know each leaf and stem
As I do. I saw them mock
My dewfall pantomime,
My scrutiny of wormcasts.

With summer came the yearning.
I skimmed mahonia beads, marked
My beaten bounds
With purple patches; but still
My airy girdle chafed, and still

Their closed world beckoned. No one
Saw my near approach, my chattering
Glide. I seized the moment
When the blue door opened wide,
And crashed into the clear sky inside.

Cats' Cradle

My mother's chair had wheels;
Her skinny arms grew big with moving it
From the bedroom to the kitchen,
Round the house and back again.

She did her gardening by proxy,
Sitting in the doorway in the sun.
While she watched she knitted,
And the two cats lay still
Among the coloured skeins
That decked her lap.

If nothing grander was on offer,
Like dancing or a day out at the races,
This is how she'd wish it:
A sunlit doorway, two contented cats
And busy fingers, an everlasting, neat
And weed-free garden.

The Disinterment of John Baskerville, Birmingham 1821

Sleeving sweaty foreheads,
They lean on shovels round the great grey box
Aslant among the uncoiled ropes,
As others prise the lid and open
An unlooked for May to Baskerville,
Dead forty years and six.

He's no eyes for it, though eyebrows,
Lashes, lips and teeth remain,
And skin as whitely perfect as his pages.
His stench sets cheesy navvies, heads askew,
Fumbling in pockets. Kerchiefs to mouth and nose,
Breath held, they thump the long night
Down on him again, the godless doom
The Bible-printer more than half believed in.

His coffin's trundled into Marston's yard
For gawping at before the furnace.
And forth it goes as plumbing, roofing, glazing;
Somewhere a line of type is spaced with lead
That held the head of Baskerville.
This is the common case, to be displaced
And lost, forgotten, although the books
That once amazed librarians remain.

Perhaps the little that was Baskerville,
Fragment of bone for future aeons to descry,
Lies where some M-way junction
Curls its petals like a concrete flower,
Or lifts its wings in amber light
Beneath an inky sky.

An Old Postcard from Lisdoonvarna

Pictures lie. These solid-seeming walls
And balconies, ornate verandas,
Were melting even then, like icing sugar
In the sea-wind's gasp, rococo iron
Shedding leprous curlicues, stucco
Unstuck, bricks ulcerated with decay.

Inside, floors sagged and took us downhill
At a trot to bed, which sagged in sympathy.
Wardrobes like mausoleums tilting
Towards the feeble light shed cones
Of woodworm dust on clothes interred
And with a groan gaped unexpectedly.

A wedding party occupied the lounge.
'Come in, come in!' they cried, conferring drinks
And sandwiches. Later we learned
What made the Irish reel. Merryman,
We thought, in his Gaelic paradise,
Would dream again, content.

With the kind of gravitas a short night earns
The summer school gathered at the bar
Before breakfast, and again at lunch,
And tea. Dinner floated in. The sun
Drew a rumpled blanket to its throat,
Collapsed unheeded in the sea.

Otherwise, there was talk, of course,
From papers and well-prepared,
Impromptu poets. What sticks now
Is the broad, white-suited back,
An arm raised gesturing, and a glass
Of red spinning in an arc.

'He speaks to the Pope for *RTE*,'
Said awed spectators. Gone, we thought,
Crusted with pink salt and ire,
Complaining to the Vatican. Fearing
An inquisition, and death by Guinness,
We packed and paid the bill, and left.

The Aquarium, Roscoff

Holiday weather: a sea-mist hangs in tatters
Over roofs a dark and lustrous blue. The street's
Old mirror, scabbed with grit, hushes fleeing cars.

No prospect of the rocky shore, too late for lunch,
We join postprandial families in the gloom,
Where, with faces etched from rock, or moulded

By a strange metallurgy, fish restlessly
Move. Our side of the glass, stone-faced humans
Jostle silently, breathing garlic-flavoured air.

An infant's voice intrudes, asserting the species' will
To recognise and name. 'Crabe,' she says, distinctly,
Pointing, 'Crabe.' Outside, the mist lifting, we wonder

At that perfect 'r' one so young is mistress of,
Beyond our mouthing, except this once, perhaps,
By pre-fixing a consonant at our command –

'Ch-rab,' we say delightedly, trying it for Frenchness;
We too are in the naming game. All, fresh as yesterday,
But thirty years ago, returned with childish voices

And a language that we do not understand.
Memories of this kind are threads that bind
Heart and tongue and mind, and us to one another.

Pond Death

At the side of the pond Steve's wall still stands;
Behind, a dead weight of clay is building.
We have seen the concrete grout between the slabs
That edge the yard above erode, the gaps begin
To grow, and now the slabs themselves aslant.
Imperceptibly, the balustrade is leaning too,
Towards the pond, as though an open hand
Were raised and slightly tilted, preparing
To let fall a load.

Time holds it struck — the clay, the slabs,
The balustrade, four feet of neatly-jointed stone —
In equipoise. This will not endure,
No more than we can last out Time;
The avalanche will sprawl its gross annihilating
Mass on pond and all.

And Steve, who mended my unlovely
Botch, rebuilt the broken wall, has gone
Already under. The dextrous hands, the eyes
That measured, the strength that weighed
And set in place that timely barricade
Are mouldering now. The bulwark, bank,
The parapet, the rampart, scarp and buttress
Of his body, insidiously mined,
Let tumult in and chaos unconfined.

The Topographical Artist

Tchaikovsky might have magnified this birth –
The twentieth of twenty-one –
With cathedral bells and cannon.
Cast out, more owl than cuckoo,
He fell softly to a sister's love,
Cherished the sense of every kind of beauty
And learned the sorrow that can bring.

I hold a vision of the Nile – pyramids, feluccas,
And the river blue beneath its cloudless sky –
On a page no bigger than my hand.
In this other Middle Eastern scene with mud-brick houses,
Palms and cliffs behind, precisely pencilled,
Among the jotted colour notes
Some muse inspired one incandescent brush stroke,
And a perfect palm-frond gleams.

How true it would have been: sand-coloured crags,
The grey and blue of distant ridges,
Simple symmetry of flat-roofed dwellings
Low and pale beneath the trees,

And Lear, all child-like laughter done,
With falling sickness, comfortless,
Round lenses gleaming in the setting sun,
Alone, his sketchbook on his knees.

Fitzrovian Follies

Mr Board, the London broadsheets say,
Is dead, the celebrated nose snuffed out
For good; the Colony has lost its light.
A line as finely spun as spittle-thread
From old soaks' lips has snapped; Fitzrovia
Is drifting out of sight, with famous drunks
From Wales, like Hamnett N and Thomas D,
Still asking for a sign we understood.

Sponging his unpaid rent, his beery fill,
Through rotting teeth and dangling cigarette
The ugly suckling rants his smutty tales.
Inflated, ill with words and booze, he beats
The dreary borderlines of louche and lewd,
Then wallows, spent, in coughs and foolishness,
Declines at last to yelping like a dog
And slides into stupor, doubly incontinent.

Feeling thirsty, naughty Nina scuffles
In her Oxo tin; short of mun, sets out
For Soho, a hoity-toity, splay-foot
Scarecrow, who dedicates her life to gin.
She leans on a crawl of bars the torso
Sculptors lusted for – Queen of Bohemia,
The sailors' friend – spills all for a bottle
And leaves a tell-tale puddle on the floor.

These two made another art of scrounging,
Cohabiting with squalor, entertained
Their friends, heedless of the price they paid
In work gone soft, not done, and bitter ends.

New York will bring DTs and doctors,
Recriminations, rivalry and rage,
A last rank sweat, while in Paddington,
Below the window, railings are waiting.

Missed Chances

My father, proto-biker,
Had leathers made for flyers,
Greatcoat, helmet, jodhpurs,
Of the First World War. His machine was olive drab,
A dinosaur. 'The old 'Arley' he called it,
A kick-start, air-cooled, 45-degree V-twin
With a twelve-horse roar that on still days
Foretold his coming by a mile or more.

His last bike he never rode,
But single-handed charmed the snarl from it again
After thirty years of silence.

We could talk that over now,
Explore the subtleties of carburettor, crankcase,
Cylinder and bore, and how the left hand
Slowly gains the right's departed lore.

Too late of course. That moment passed
Before I learned to ask and listen,
Ask again, lest conversation perish
On the sudden, final closing of the door.

Baskerville's Milton, 1758

I can read the text at five feet,
In good light, though only sense
Distinguishes long-s from f,
(Much the same, God knows, at two),
But would not for pride's sake forgo
The weight of this great quarto
In the hand and that stale tobacco whiff
From two centuries of smoky rooms.

Five dukes subscribed and fourteen
Belted earls, any number of barts.,
And bishops, fells. of that college
And this; one Copelstone
Warre Bampfylde, Esquire, artist;
A Darwin (Erasmus), M.D., still young,
Who cared no more for peers
Than the type founder; Benj. Franklin,
Also Esq., of Philadelphia,
Republican and quondam friend,
Who thought the letter strokes so thin,
Their narrowness fatigued the eyes.
Philadelphia's literate preferred
Their printing squat, like their journalists.

But the scrivener's son, his light unspent,
Would have approved this Latin alphabet
For Satan's mutiny, man's fall from grace,
Types as precise and shapely as his lines,
The pamphleteer and regicide allowed
A master of mechanic arts to curse
The wickedness of priests, and from the grave
Abjure us to emancipate our minds
From superstition and servility.

Lamb liked Milton for supper reading,
With Gloucester cheese and a smoke.
Fatty crumbs of recognition
Would have gladdened Baskerville,
Whose diet was the weasel words
Of tight-fisted academics:
Praise and payment both were balm indeed.

He sold out to the French,
Who have an eye for elegance
And can spot a bargain from afar.
Is some stitch lacking
In the garment of our island soul?
Milton, spurred by fame alone,
Sold his copyright 'for not above ten pounds',
While a treatise on the game of whist
Brought Mr Hoyle two hundred.

Jackdaws

I've tried curses, but they lack the Prelate's
Power of blasting feathers, and shooing them
Betsy Trotwood-like will only work
Outside the house; they see me rattle
Windows at them and they know I'm caged.

'Chop, chop!' they cry, joshing one another,
And since they've shown the full-fledged young
The knack, short of cannon, nothing will succeed.
It was envy of those gaudy acrobats
The jays, taking more than any dozen tits

And finches, that taught my fiends the trick.
Jays are easy on the eye and pay their way,
But jackdaws in their mourning black and grey,
With that evil, pearly eye, are not my love.
Besides, I have a distant memory

Of waking in pale dawn, a terrifying rush
Of pinions round my head and blackness
Frantic at the curtains – and of the buckets
Full of sticks and pegs and sheep's wool cleared
The previous day, to let the chimney breathe.

And here again they'd settled – *demi-pension*:
Twigs from the trees, moss from the garden wall,
And a daily food supply laid out for them.
That their nesting might have suffocated us
Did not occur. 'Ciao! Ciao!' they greet their friends

From neighbour roofs and in a clan descend to feed.
I can reach the chimney too, and break the nest,
But that black, appalling, naked chick that yawned
Its dreadful mouth to me is stuck now
In the gallery of my guilt and won't be moved.

Bed and Breakfast
in the Berkshires, Mass.

O, Molly G. what a welcome you gave us –
Of scrawled notes with few directions more than
'Help yourselves'. And what surprises too,
As open-mouthed we saw the Piranesis
In the study, Le Corbusier, Picasso,

Blake and Arp and Calder up the stairs,
Escher tucked away in corners, and in your room,
Where other paying guests might themselves
Have drawn a line, the sombre Vlaminck
Landscape thundering above your bed.

At breakfast more notes, but not one that told
How to make the toaster toast, and the Berkshires'
Biggest ants that tumbled in the dish
With Cheerios and fled across the cloth,
The hoard of bottles where we sought the trash.

And surprises still that last day: you there
In your backyard, a clearing in the woods,
And the shock of gaudy hollyhocks
From seeds your sister stole in Monet's garden,
'Like this,' you added, shaking handfuls out,

'Take them home.' If we'd had Molly's skill
Something of Giverny might have grown with us.
But she left no directions, and now we hear
She's gone. As the adage has it, art survives,
But, when nights draw in, it will not ward off loneliness.

Maître Jacques

Our old Breton friends, sentenced to six months
Each year selling onions door-to-door,
Lived on little, in no style. Maître Jacques,
Compatriot, had style enough and a way with duck,

Spatchcocked and crisp-baked, he had not learned
At home. It brought him customers
From Francestown and scattered homesteads
Miles around, and never just for once.

He profited in friends as much as cash,
But still sang of his *bro*, and would, he said,
Go back. His New Hampshire fields and woods
He loved. Walking his land one late October day,

The fall leaves mush beneath his feet,
Lone figure as the dusk began to thicken,
He did not hear, three hundred yards away,
The rustle as a hunter drew a bead.   .

To My Namesake

When, greener than most, I packed the trunk
For college, I had no need to change
The name or the address inside. Though printed
In your hand more than twenty years before,
Both were as surely mine as they had been yours.

I lay beside my mother on the day you died,
Making no sense of life beyond milk
And the first web strands of the love that binds,
Knowing nothing of the teatime jokes
And laughter that was your last of family.

And now, sixty years on, I learn our trunk
Went with you to Italy, heavier
Than it should have been: the gifts of clothes
From corner shops to poor relations
Neatly buttoned with half-sovereigns.

Smuggler, then, you were, but for your friends,
Helping their profits homewards.
(Whether Mussolini got them in the end
Is best not thought about.) Perhaps you sang
On boat and train the hymns you sang at work,

That in the pit's black anonymity
Told colliers of your coming and unleashed
A cheerful counterpoint of mandrel thuds
And rattling shovels, 'Onward Christian
Soldiers' echoing all along the face.

And what did they make of you, Salvationist,
In Italy, when our trunk gave up its gold?
With few English words of greeting, and no Welsh,
What could they do but lay out sunshine and ripe fruit
For you, and make a welcome voluble with signs and smiles?

Swimming in the Red Sea

And so I swam, weightless, such little wavering
Effort of my flippered feet, parting of bubble
Trails with my strangely white hands, life gathered
In the slow moving shadow on the whiter sand:

Fish, multitudinous and bright, such undreamed
Colours, I would have rubbed my eyes but the glass said
No. I should have shouted my amazement –
Nought but the gargled monotone of each long

Breath spoke. Fingers of coral grasped at me,
Knuckles of coral gleamed, the lucent core
Of coral minds throbbed. Shoals circled ocean poles
Endlessly, familiar beings in their element.

The space of water widened, my feebly moving
Shade another patch of wrinkled sand.
A blue opacity hung from the gleaming
Wavelets, down to the bluer depths. Sterterous

Each liquid breath, and my body, cold, rolled
Laboriously and turned, as it will always
Hope to turn, back from the beckoning gloom
To the shallows' peopled luminosity.

Karpaz Peninsula

The road descends the ridge from Dipkarpaz
Holding the handle's underside, the shaft of Cyprus
Tilting to the east and north. There Anatolia's
Shoulder hangs protectively. Mid-course for Roman Patras

And martyrdom as monstrous as his brother's,
Andrew beached here, where his God, or one familiar
With the coast, told him water for the voyage
Could be found. All is Allah's lordship now:

The crops, the black-robed women bowed beneath their loads,
Smiling children waving, men at tric-trac in the shade.
The monastery, deserted, sulks in heat.
A grey cat sprawls asleep; only a vast sow

Slowly moves, her silhouetted dugs like teeth
Are set to saw the dust. An armed guard bars the cape,
That fingerpost to Antioch; we take the church
Instead – Apostolos Andreas, his church,

Iconostasis, brass and polished wood.
In prayer to him the faithful piled these waxen
Limbs and viscera, mimetic offerings
Of thanks for saintly intercession, or to beg

Release from pain. Is this the end of our journey –
A silent, empty church, these pallid fragments?
Is there no answer at the frontier of belief,
As the burnished sea beats on a broken land?

War Casualty

These late September, cloud-bleared skies, this first
Autumnal chill, recall that wartime caravan
Behind the dunes, the empty beach, black rocks
At the white edge of the sea – and a mother's pain
Of loneliness with her child, its thin limbs flailing,
Like a broken toy, but never winding down.

Each day that week, between showers and tides,
I tended the rock pool, stocked its silent world
With shells and shellfish, displayed beneath its glaze
Anemones in clusters, while in the deeps
Of a distant sea, the bones of sailors,
Swaying, swaying, made what they could of love.

And, at night, swaddled in the heavy shawl,
Never lulled by the wind's gentle rocking
Of the van, senseless to the sea's ceaseless
Hush upon the shore, the rain's sudden drumming,
The child fought sleep, its cries rising and falling,
Piercing the thin walls and heedless dark.

Cathédrale St-Étienne, Bourges

The town is pinned in place by this vast peg.
From its crown the knitting of ten thousand roofs
Unravels into broader thoroughfares,
And distantly the river curves. How could man think this,

And then build his thought, without a host
Of angels bearing hods? Four hundred weary
Steps above the floor the tower gestures
Finialed arabesques of stone to heaven.

Beneath the floor, below gem-pierced walls
And apses, in a pall of dust the masons
Saw their distant homes recede. Stone their medium
And calling, they dwelt in it, etched the morrow's plans

On stone, cracked jokes with a chisel. On springers
Of ogive vaulting so precise the heart leaps,
They cut man in all his randy foolishness:
So close to God, so far from his angels.

Davies the Agent

'Dafydd Ffossil', pit-boy at twelve, swinging
The doors that sprang the hauliers and their teams
Clamouring into light, saw in the drams
Of waste the world's longest autumn petrified.

Manager of men, he fought the fire that killed them,
And summoned troops to fight their fire within.
Little worse for that, he descended into dark,
And traced the seams that paid in steam and steel.

They became collectors too. Among his cabinets
Of specimens are some that bear, beside the black lead
Gloss of foliage, *cordaites* or *pecopteris*,
The dusty thumbprint of my grandfather.

Across the cwm, above the noise and smoke,
Three first-floor windows of the agent's house
Give back the sun. But Davies is not there.
On a distant hillside, below an ice field's

Salt and silver, a song died on his lips,
And he was added to that great catalogue
Of organisms folded into earth.
His headstone should impress, if not his bones on clay,

His life on memory. Beyond our garden gate
The pit had spilled a library of dog-eared tomes.
We would split their folios for images of plants,
Each one original, for all time perfected.

'Al Alvarez will be 70 on Tuesday'
(*Observer*)

We go a long way back, Al, you and I.
In truth, I hardly know you, though we've shared
Moments intimes we'd normally reserve
For wives. We once sat naked together –
On a slatted bench, sipping Finnish beer.
Sweat dripped, you smoked your pipe and smiled, Buddha-
Like, I thought, said little, seemed interested
In the *soi-disant* second-best Swedish
Poet in Finland.
            Still naked, we ran
The thirty yards downhill to hit the lake,
And wondered why the instant icy shock
We feared withheld itself. Perhaps numbness
Supervened.
          A paparazzo's grainy
Black and white will prove we slept together,
Outdoors in Lahti. Multilingual cans
Pressed to our ears, eyes closed, we concentrate
On vacancy. No, I'll grant your restless
Mind remained alert. Cannot say the same
For mine. If you've forgotten that northern
Summer, this memory's my gift to you.
It's late I know, but happy birthday, Al.

Digs at 'Glenhuntley'

Whoever named the house, its bow windows
Peering out of the line of terrace, must have had
Ambition to catch the early tourist
Up for the season, when Aber had ambition;
Perhaps the canny Cardi sort who kept its secret –
A whitewashed longhouse from the days of fields
Before Bridge Street – as carefully hidden
As his language, out the back, beside his own
Few square yards of flags and open fire.

In our daft pupillage, the fifties, Mrs D,
Whose every move suggested sapless wood
And clumsy hands still unfamiliar with the strings,
Conceded bed and breakfast from her small, stiff grasp
Like charity. Our expectations were as mean:
What if ablutions were Victorian, bacon arrived
Barely coloured from the gas, and evening
Found us crouched about the hearth in overcoats?
The front room, its funereal prints, immortelles,
Stuffed creatures under glass, proscribed as rigidly
As warmth, we viewed outside, distorted through its bull's eye
Panes. What distortion Mrs D could see in us
God knows, as her thick lenses scrutinised
The deviant microbe in our souls for signs of growth.

We learned the trick from her, watched her husband
Flinch and roll anywhere away when her goggles
Flashed. His spouseless sister, fleshy-soft like him
To her sharp stick, smiled only when alone.
And the sister's daughter? Ah, the surly Ann,
Little more than child when we arrived,
Was less than woman still when we first heard

The muffled grapplings, dark in the hall
Outside our narrow door – and, later, weeping.
Time brought around exams, intenser whisperings
About the house, and school skirts widening
At the waist. We made good our get away.

I saw her only once again. Wedded
In the vac (of course), and aged by more than months,
She wheeled a shabby pram up Darkgate Street.
At the fag-end of our days of indiscretion
Glenhuntley's door had closed on all of us.

'The Maesglas Marciano'
(i.m. Dick Richardson 1934–1999)

We're of an age, but while you roughed it up
From street-fighter to pro, I shadow-boxed with life.
I watched you in that makeshift gym on stilts above the sea
Rehearsing for the thousandth time, speedball, heavy-bag,

Three sharp rounds, and the classiest skipping
I'd ever seen, rope a blur, machine-gun rapping
On the wooden floor and feet so light they could have trod
The tide beneath. That was when you knocked out

Sixteen has-beens and hopefuls in as many months
To earn those pay-days in Dortmund, Gothenburg,
Porthcawl. Headstrong dealer in scars and blunt intentions,
You left your mark on Cooper's brow, gave once

The crowd at Coney Beach two brawls for a ticket,
And lost a date with 'Big Cat' from the States
When his God stepped in to stop the match.
And now the papers say Cleveland Williams too,

Another of our vintage, has taken
His final tumble, across the bonnet
Of a speeding car, who should have been yours
That night, twelve years and a kidney fitter

Than when Ali sent him reeling to his corner,
Coughing blood. We all go privately
In our different ways: Ali shuffling slowly
To his maker, Williams suddenly, walking

From dialysis to a busy street,
And you from cancer's body-blows. I think
Of you, fancy skipper, hope my footwork
Keeps me out of range another while.

Sirmione '99

All that is known of the lyric poetry of Gaius Valerius Catullus (c.84–54 BC) derives from transcripts of a single MS said to have been discovered at the end of the 13th century in Verona, the poet's birthplace, where it was being used as the bung for a wine-barrel. Many of his poems tell of his passionate love for Lesbia, and his later disillusionment. He had a villa at Sirmione, now a tourist resort on Lake Garda.

I

At breakfast, over-dressed, smiling waiters
Wipe sweat from hands and well-shaved upper-lips.
Denied the pleasures of her ample breasts,
Lesbia's sparrows importune the other guests.

II

Later we see her saunter by with Mercury.
In vain (for vanity) blue sandal-straps,
Untied, flutter at ankles, for he's held,
Doomed to the prospect of this dusty strand
By Lesbia's promise and her small moist hand.

III

Lesbia in a one-piece, white, splashes
To the shallows, ungainly hoists herself
But fails to sit, sprawls backwards on the side,
Lips parted, arms and legs (alas) spread wide.

Her lover casts about the pool and hooks
The dark-glazed eyes of sundry men, who watch
Intrigued her bounteous form, for all displayed,
As though she practised woman's oldest trade.

IV

Heat vibrating from the harbour's paving
Wafts a caress up tawny Lesbia's thighs,
A sight enough to set old men raving,
And stir the young as rotting meat does flies
To a fever of tumescent craving,
And then to hopelessness and feeble sighs,
For Lesbia's teasing fingers stroke her swain,
Whose proud neck arches to her touch again.

Unable to resist, he cups his hands
Round the sprung contours of her soft behind,
Envious of convention's harsh commands
Longs for her ample body unconfined,
Wishes the ferry queue on other strands,
All eyes save his and hers at once struck blind.
So, fixed they stand like figures carved in gesso,
While he awaits his *biglietto ingresso*.

(After James Michie's translation of Catullus)

Humfrey Lhuyd's Last Adieu

(A found poem)

Humphrey Lhuyd (c.1527–1568), the antiquary and map–maker, was born in Denbigh and educated at Oxford University. He produced the first map of Wales as a separate country, and one of England and Wales, published post–humously in 1573. Lhuyd's friendship with the Dutch geographer, Abraham Ortelius, extended over many years. Their correspondence was conducted in Latin, also the language of the fragmentary historical and geographical descrip–tion of Britain which, with his maps, Lhuyd sent to Ortelius from his deathbed. Thomas Twyne translated the *Commentarioli Descriptionis Britannicae Fragmentum* into English and when, in 1573, he published his translation as *The Breuiary of Britayne*, it was accompanied by Lhuyd's last letter to Ortelius (the spelling preserved from the original text):

To the Most adorned, and best deseruynge to be reuerenced
of al that loue the knowledge of the Mathematicks,
Abraham Ortelius of Andwarp.

Dearly beloued *Ortelius*,
that day wherein I was constrayned to depart
from *London*: I receyued your Description of ASIA:
and before I came home to my house:
I fell into a very perillous Feuer,
which hath so torne this poore body of mine,
these x. continuall dayes: that I was brought
into despayre of my life. But, my hope
Iesus Christe, is layde vp in my bosome.
Howbeit, neither the dayly shakynge
of the continuall Feuer, with a double
Tertian, neither the lookyng for present death,

neither the vehement headache without
intermission: could put the remembrance
of my *Ortelius*, out of my troubled brayne.
Wherefore, I send unto you my *Wales*,
not beutifully set forth in all poyntes,
yet truly depeinted, so that certeyn
notes be observed, which I gathered
euen when I was redy to die.

You shall also receaue the description
of *England*, set forth as well with the auntient
names: as those which are now used, and an other
England also drawne forth perfectly enough. Besides
certein fragmentes written with mine owne hande.
Which, notwithstandynge that they be written foorth
in a rude hande, and seeme to be imperfect:
yet doubt not, they be well grounded by proofes,
and authorities of auntient writers.

Which also (if God had spared me life)
you should have receaved in better order,
and in all respects perfect. Take therfore,
this last remembrance of thy *Humfrey*,
and for ever *adieu*, my deare friend *Ortelius*.

From *Denbigh*, in *Gwynedh*, or *North Wales*,
the .xxx. of August, 1568.

Yours both liuyng, and diying:
Humfrey Lhuyd.

42

Lieutenant Jahleel Brenton Carey
Hears of the Death
of Prince Louis Napoleon, 2 June 1879

I'd watched Papa, the third Napoleon, crack
In the grip of Bismark and his generals,
And here was Lou-Lou, his great-uncle's sword
At Austerlitz to goad him in his pack,
And not a soul with sense to rein him back.

Some high-born madman let him take the trip,
Too hot for Prince Imperial, or English gent
Who thinks Zulus better sport than foxes,
Decisions made with saddle, spurs and whip,
And military tactics only horsemanship.

I'd seen Isandhlwana, seen the evil sprawl
Of gutted soldiers. The Zulu had refined
The art of war, you handled him with care:
Louis led our troopers to the empty kraal,
And stretched out for a smoke beside the wall.

To be fair, he never cared for rank or class,
Enjoyed discussing Bonaparte's campaigns.
The men boiled coffee; he did not set a guard,
To see, without a breeze, a ripple pass
A chain away in tall tambookie grass.

A solitary Zulu on a rise
Some distance off propelled us to our feet,
Scrambling towards the horses and our arms.
'Prepare to mount,' called Louis. Bright surprise
Of glory seemed to dawn, but glory lies.

Before the second order came, dread
Hell broke loose – shots from the giant grass, figures
Leaping out, yells, hide shields, black spear-arms raised.
I dug my spurs, the whole world lurched, we fled
The kraal along the dried-up river bed.

You say he failed to mount. How could we have known
His horse took fright and bolted? You say he caught a strap,
It snapped, he fell beneath the flailing hooves,
They slashed his sword-arm, gashing to the bone.
Great God, I see him struggle to his feet and stand alone.

In dreams I can't escape the vision, must
I, waking, witness him at bay, unable to resist,
A bloody mist spraying the trampled grass,
The hope of half of France, her lingering lust
For Empire, dribbling in Africa's dust.

Images of the Writer–Artist

In clouds of stench and stumbling shards of stone
Like mounds of broken lace, he watched
A line of *poilus* laid as on parade, heads back
Feet bare, unshaven faces grey, eyes rolling
Or already blank. By each in turn
The soutane smudged the dust; the knife
In fingers deft with oysters prised the jaw
To take the sacrament – last rites
Without compunction. No saving work
For ambulance; brushing his couture
Uniform, he turned aside.

Later, smiling zouaves (welcomed
To the only *douche* for miles along the Somme,
His lens a penis eye) he saw melted
In mud to teeth and spikes of bone.
Such waste of lovely men his suave soul wept –
Oh for peace, for poetry, the *corps de ballet*,
Art. Like Orpheus ascended to Montmartre,
He charmed and edited the avant-garde.

And later still his sculptured nostrils caught
The reek of boxers in the gym. Sweat-polished
Limbs and torsos held his eyes. He soaped himself
A poem in bathwater one saved for him.

Day-trip from Paris to Le Havre

Never saw the like: a garland, spun bouquet
Of women, black, and for the day
Coiffed and draped from neck to sandaled feet,
Gay as birds of paradise or fairground carousels.

The board-walk over pebbles
Snakes its scales, rocking them gently,
Gently to the sea.
Waves withdraw with customary hush,
Gather a puny surge to wash
Over toes and ankles, knees
And so on up, till gorgeous hues
Flower about them, head-dress stamens
Bow together in the breeze.

Five. Coaches at the kerbside grumble,
Search-parties spill out – and disappear,
Exactly as the Gauloise-puffing drivers fear.

The stray – a young man almost certainly,
Playing volley-ball with locals, sharing a drink or three,
Fallen over untied trainer laces,
Slow to disengage from hot embraces.

Or, along the margin of the pebbly shore,
Some self-absorbed and hugely-petalled flower drifts,
While families from the beach huts
Wave a thousand *tricolores* and cheer.

A Triptych
(i.m. Joan, 1921–1999)

I

Lungs awash, mind at fox-trot with fever,
My sister gazed through me to the window
And the roof beyond. 'Those birds don't fly away,'
She said. 'See them there . . . three — all the time.'

Vultures, I thought, scanning slate for a patch
Of moss, some aliform quirk of ridge-tile
That might explain her vision. There was none.
But she didn't die. After the beaded illnesses

Of a childhood whose earliest memory
Was of our weeping parents kneeling
At her cot, there seemed left no dying
In her: another daft illusion.

II

Sweeping leaves, bristle brash on stone,
Recalled a distant square-cut floor,
Twitch of hay from rack, rhythm of bran
And oats and, once, in gloom beyond half-door,

A foal, first legs splayed, rocking
Gently in the mare's sweet breath,
Myself to brush piss-yellow straw hock
Deep and great brown turds beneath

The pony's dripping teats. She turned
Her bulging eye on me, eased me to the wall
And held me, while my boyhood burned,
Helpless till my sister heard my call.

III

I wouldn't claim that he had crossed himself,
But Jordan too is dead, and little mourned.
Unwanted guard-dog with a bouncer's build,
He would groan for love, insinuate his haunch

Beneath a hand that might, however
Thoughtlessly, caress. His leap was terrible.
The chance reflection of a watch-glass
On the wall awoke in him God knows what atavistic

Threat of torchlight in a darkened room
That drove him to a frenzy, foam splashing
From his mantrap jaws. Alone my sister,
Not much more that half his bulk, could curse

His madness to a whimpering stop.
When she died, his well of rough affection
Sealed, he turned morose, took to walks alone
And chasing after cars. Within a month

They found him crammed into a corner, eyes
Fixed as on a roaming light, teeth bared against the world.

Uncles

Leslie Gilmore

   – learned his trade at nautical college in the dah-dit
    days of glowing valves and stuttering key, blessed
    Marconi for a life above the ground and took himself
    to sea. 'Can you be a gentleman?' the captain asked.
    The reply came pat and he was officer class, the sickest
    seaman in the merchant fleet.

   – weathered, just, the storms of Far East voyages, had his fill
    and more of a world that ended at a ship's rail, hankered
    for a space where the horizon knew its place, the throb
    of engines stopped and great waves hammering
    'Let me in' on plates.

   – quit his berth at Freemantle: landlegs and companions
    found, bought himself a horse and swag and set off east.
    The Nullarbor empty as Eyre had left it eighty years before,
    arid days of unblemished blue, saltbush and solitary trees
    half-flayed in heat, his friends turned back. But, for him,
    the horizon held steady and hugely distant, the trail
    buzzed in the wind straight as telegraph wire.

   – followed black poles tailing to an exclamation mark
    every day and the next, ignoring the Southern Ocean
    and the Bight's great cliffs, to Eucla, where a sudden fig-tree
    bound a rock with roots like crippled fingers and the repeater
    station hummed a promise, and on again, at last to Adelaide.

   – finished her in Sydney. The reason for his journey falling
    into place, built a transmitter and morsed a message.
    Far out on the Pacific a hand replied, 'Congratulations.'

His prize, the keys to a station on a tropic isle, 16 S 167 E:
New Hebrides.

– blessed Cook and Bougainville, added to his lingos French
  and pidgin, unlearned the tidiness his mother taught
  (left it all to servants), married a planter's widow,
  gained a mother-in-law who'd counted bar-takings
  in sacklets of dust and nuggets.

– sent Christmas cards, came back once to tell his tale,
  said his goodbyes and vanished from our lives.

Hubert and Cyril

– had birth dates unnaturally close and were not twins,
  nor alike, except in being boys together at the fag-end of ten,
  the younger dark-haired and oddly tall.

Which pushed the terrier? Saw the dog's rump raised, its stump
of tail a-tremble as, chin on paws, it watched stones drop
down the shaft and, muttering perhaps, 'Go on then, after them,'
pushed; or did it slip and, short legs flailing, fall? Both boys ran.

In their shared bed that night, awake, they heard barking faint
and distant, whispered together, rose stealthily in darkness, dressed
and crept outside to the mountain and the ring of broken brick
that topped the old pit-mouth, listened in the silence
to its secret waters trickling, whistled, called the dog.

Echo or wind in old workings far below said something
was alive. Hubert, the smaller, squirmed backwards through
the hole, sought a foothold, lost his grip and fell
twelve feet to the first criss-crossing girder, stuck there.
Immense pain held him fast.

Months later, hip mended, he began a limping life. Still young,
the friend of bigger men, he learned to lose his feebleness
in bars, started fights that others finished. A henpecked
husband, distanced from companions, frail, he would lean
on his stick distracted, as one listening for a distant sound.

Cyril charmed animals, convinced my sister that the spider
he fed with wingless flies came at his voice and had golden
eyes. Cats coiled about his ankles, snakes twined inside his shirt,
dogs and horses waited on his word. Girls soon fell as easily
to his spell. He courted with a blanket on his arm: 'Love by name,
love by nature,' he said and smiled.

After dances he pocketed white gloves and bared his fists,
defending balls and profile in a ring of outraged suitors,
floored once a six-foot-four policeman who'd sworn
he'd wipe the smile and fix the cocky son for good.

He might have cut a swathe through the womanhood
of Rhondda, but the war quenched half his spirit. On leave
he came black-bereted, armed, moustached like Errol Flynn,
in time survived Dieppe and, Hitler done, tried keeping shop
and bartending.

Women came and went, till Peggy threatened suicide and cowed him
to the registrar. Soon after, too, she stabbed him. Divorced, his spark
all but gone out, he dwindled to a south-coast hideaway. Strange,
and stranger: dead, he was my mother's nephew and I not his.

B&B in the White Mountains, Arizona

Stepping-stones across the bridgeless
Little Colorado are designed to tilt.
We dry out on the stiff trail through the woods,
Littered with rocks and fallen branches
Stalking like insects, to sunlit meadows,
Where showers of aspen coins
Pretend a new mythology.

The sun declines to stay. We start
The long trek back,
Down to the Little Colorado,
Wet our feet again.

Charles and Mary have the sturdy corpulence
Of well-nourished pioneers.
They might have entered this high valley
On a wagon train, felled the timber
For their lodge. They keep a strict regime:
Don't expect to eat if you miss
The breakfast call. Clocks take turns
To chime. In small wooden bedrooms
Guests spend sleepless hours
Thinking of premature burial.

Outside, the night is crystalline.
The Great Bear leans against a tree
Across the road; a sheen of frost
Caps fence posts, stiffens each blade of grass;
The river stands for a molten moment
Still in a vacant beaver dam.

Night Ride

We might have forgone Taos,
The rotten road to Lobo Mountain,
Spiralling dust behind, the steep ascent
To the whitewashed
Sentry-box in its resinous shade;
Still better, gone without
A BLT and fries at Bloomfield
As night fell on the desert;
But with the snow-spatted pines
Of the Rockies behind
And New Mexico's eateries few
And very far between, and closing early,
It seemed an OK thing to do.

Shiprock put the Indian sign on us,
Its main drag bending left
As the 64 goes right:
The Navajo's revenge.
In moonless black we hummed oblivious
Straight down route 666.

Speed mesmerized, we saw bright eyes
On distant hills abruptly vanish
To reappear much closer, whooshing by
Like wandering souls.
The sudden lights of Gallup, sixty miles
Out of our way, we thought the worst of dreams –
But we were wrong.

The nightmare was the shape
That rose an hour later, plumb in the road ahead,
Ghost buffalo or ox, domestic cow,

And sped towards us.
The braking shudder of the Chevrolet
Explained the twin side-winding trails
Black on daylit empty highways.

That ended conversation
And left us darkling with the dashboard lights,
The only sound the motor's drone.

Bryce, Utah

The motel sits on a prehistoric beach
Where deer and bobcat bones and flakes of flint
Rejected by arrow-head quality control
Mingle with stumble brush and shingle.

A cautionary catalogue of don'ts
Enjoins the carefree traveller to keep
His door secure. For the first time
In this ghastly aftermath we feel unsafe.
But morning comes blue and bright
With tumbled bins, litter, wind
Or raccoon strewn, and water
In our booze-box turned again to ice.

Perhaps we missed another monitory
Sign: 'Avoid our Dog House Diner;
Go to Ruby's half-mile up the road'.
Once inside, alone, between the giant-screen TV
And a king-sized quilting frame,
We feel obliged to stay, and duly fail to eat
The worst breakfast in the South-West USA.

The canyon's carved from ice-cream,
Pink and white, melting swiftly still in earth-time.
Dramatic curtains, temples, pinnacles and spires
Are tottering as we look. But paths are hard beneath
Our feet and pines bolt skywards from bare rock.

Mules peck and slither dainty down
The narrow, winding trail,
Never more than inches from the edge.

The saddle galls the rider
Not the beast. Down at last,
In file among the trees, comes
A momentary illusion of old West.

Back at the Lodge, we visit Ebenezer Bryce,
Totem stiff in sepia. Mormon pioneer,
At whatever distance, Welshman:
We doff our baseball caps.

A Fresh Start

Colour had left him, draining
From within.
                    Dina took off
Her clothes, lay down on the sofa,
Her arms, her legs, her torso
Thus and thus and thus, and smiled.
The old man searched and found
A sketchbook, pen and ink,
And his wax-pale hand caressed
The paper.
              Still smiling, Dina
Turned; she moved her arms,
Her legs, her torso, thus and thus
And thus. And the old man's hand
Moved swiftly with a tiny susurrus.
The pen forgot to hesitate, encircling
Her wrist and throat with beads,
And Dina smiled. 'You know
I cannot stay,' she murmured. 'Bonnard
Needs me, standing in his bathroom. He says
His painting's stalled.'
                        'Bugger Bonnard,'
The old man whispered in his beard,
Then quietly, aloud, 'Raise your arms
Above your head, and stretch
That foot a little – yes.' And his hand
Flew over the page.
                    And they stopped,
For Dina was thirsty, and drank
A little wine. The old man's fingers,
Trembling slightly, stroked

The glass and placed it on the table
Thus. And he looked at her.

And Dina, smiling, dropped her wrap
And lay down on the sofa.

(In the early 1940s, Aristide Maillol, the sculptor, asked his favourite model, Dina Vierny, to pose for his friends, Matisse, who had been seriously ill, and Bonnard, who had lost his wife and muse. Matisse, inspired again, produced a series of exquisite pen and ink drawings.)

Bomb on Gilfach

Not meant to be the target, we copped a stray.
When Swansea burned and set the sky alight,
Some German aircraft, limping loaded from the fray,
Fleeing shattered streets, dismembered dead,
Droned on and onwards through a moonless night.
The pilot, frantic for a fix, and the valleys' spread
Fingers black on black beneath, said,
'Drop the poxy thing, we're losing height.'

A bomb fell in the night and no one died.
The news arrived as fat bacon fried
For breakfast with yesterday's damped bread:
The doctor's surgery was smashed, they said,
The old man, wrapped in wool and flannelette,
Descended safe abed through splintered planks
To the floor below. The windows of the church were blank;
Entire its slated roof had shifted
As if a clumsy hand had lifted
And once more, at an angle, set

It down. The war had come to seek us out
And we had slept. Some evil Nazi lout
Had dropped a bomb a few yards from our door
And no one heard. But all our nights were full
Of lumbering drams, the thump and roar
Of engines, infernal rattles as the coal was screened.
We would start to wakefulness if a lull
Occurred and somehow silence supervened.

Behind the skew-whiff church and silenced bell,
On a rushy patch of moss and water seep,
A vast inverted cone of mud struck deep
Into the hill. The frogs had been through hell.
We searched and fought for jagged shards
Of bomb, swapping spares for sets of cards
Or stamps – and watched them rust on windowsills;
Most wonderful, the doctor's cellar door, blown down,
Disclosed his scattered packs of bandages and pills,
And, lustrous in the sunlight, carboys, blue and brown.

At the Spanish Steps

February again, late afternoon:
Black fingers tilt
The fountain's silver, quick
In its marble spoon.
Sun stripes spilt
From a shadowed alley
Across the cobbled square
Will not linger there.
Darkness follows soon.

Severn, sentry in the march
Of life, saw the fountain,
Like a foundered boat, lurch
At its mooring. Light ebbing,
Descended the steep stair, ran
One thirty steps across the square, sobbing,
To the trattoria,
Bought supper for a dying man.

Six sentry paces past the narrow cot,
Two at the blank wall,
Six paces back, turn,
Three at the tall,
Shuttered windows. Look down:
There in the marble hull,
Like blood, the waters for a moment burn.

After the death mask,
The scissored curl of auburn hair,
After the bonfire, the sickbed burned to ash,
After the vengeful smash
Of unflawed pots, the room waits,
Still at last, stripped bare.

And troupes of lovers pass
To climb the steps and meet
With others going down, or pause
To sit and lean together, close.
Water in the wallowing boat
Catches a gleam, holds it afloat.

Like Severn, I see the sun's snail track
Recede across the water's black,
Walk six paces back.

Beaux Arts

I Beatrice Hastings

Bea hunted Paris like the old Transvaal:
Men and women notched her bedpost like a rasp.
Modigliani, who adored her bare,
Dressed her in paint for the Quat'z'arts Ball,
Orage held her in his hot New Age grasp;
Picasso procured her for Apollinaire –
On leave; Pound adored her for a time,
And Lewis worshipped at her slippery shrine.
You ask what happened in the end
To Beatrice, the artists' friend,
Journalist, pianist, latterly souse.
See her kneeling at the open oven door,
Cushion for her head, blanket on the floor,
And, in her hand, a pet white mouse.

(Beatrice Hastings (Emily Alice Haigh), writer, 1879-1943)

II Marie Vassilieff

Marie makes every night a party
At her studio canteen, for the thirsty and sad,
For the artists and the arty,
The narcissistic and plain mad.
She dances for anyone who'll wish,
Dances most with Leon Trotsky,
Dances the Cossack 'dance of the fish'.
Eternal woman, cares for all
In Montparnasse, knows how to feed and mend
Those bandaged bloodily, how to tend
Weeping stumps and weeping, broken men.
And she is, oh, so small:
How does she strive and bend
Unendingly, with the strength of ten?

(Marie Vassilieff, artist, 1884-1957)

III Jean Cocteau (double exposure)

See dandy Cocteau loiter there,
See him all elegance even then,
In the shambles of a ruined town,
Uniform à la mode, rouged cheeks, curled hair,
His black malacca poised to pick
A way through blasted stone, stained glass and brick
'Like a mountain of old lace,' he told a friend;
See him pause and frown.
He snaps the lens of those bold dark eyes
On priest prising the jaws of dying men,
Who receive the Host, whether they would or no,
And sighs the most fastidious of sighs:
Such lamentable absence of punctilio.
See him shudder, turn his head and go.

Here's Cocteau at the front again, the Somme
This time, still ambulance man
Extraordinaire, opening his van,
Welcoming Zouaves and Senegalese
To take a shower oft as they please,
Away from the chaos of mud, shell and bomb,
While he plays the supplicant on his knees,
Camera suspended twixt finger and thumb.
So much for the war. He'll leave the campaign
For writing and art, black boxers, cocaine.
Hence clogging fatigue and lustreless eyes,
Aux armes! avant-garde, and praise to the skies.
When all's said and done, he's much more at home,
Parading with Diaghilev in Rome.

(Jean Cocteau, writer, artist, film-maker, 1889-1963)